NEVER GIVE UP!
The Story of a 21st Century Yogini

Illustrated by: Gabo Giacopello
Tashi Paldron

Published by

OWL PUBLISHERS

www.owlpublishers.com
360 S Market St, San Jose, CA 95113,
United States.

Printed in the United States of America

INTRODUCTION

Have you ever been at a crossroads in your life where you were ready to give up?

I walk a path shaped by devotion, discipline, and discovery. My journey began not with grand visions, but with a quiet longing to understand myself and the world around me. Through meditation, study and self-reflection, I found a way to transform challenges into teachers and silence into wisdom.

Life has offered me moments of struggle and renewal, each one guiding me deeper into my truth, revealing that peace is not found outside, but cultivated within. Meditation became more than a practice—it became my way of living, a sacred thread weaving together body, speech and mind.

Along the way, I learned that surrender is strength, compassion is power, and authenticity is freedom. My story is not about perfection, but about embracing the sacred in everyday life and walking with courage toward the light.

This book is my offering to the world: a space where I share my journey, my practices, and my heart, so that others may find inspiration to walk their own path of awakening.

TABLE OF CONTENTS

This story begins in Mexico City at the end of the 1960s, where I grew up in a loving, protective, non-Christian family while searching for my spiritual path.

My intention is to open my heart to you. Regardless of what you choose to believe, each of us has an extraordinary story to tell. My wish is that by sharing what I consider to be my truth through memories from my life, I will inspire and benefit others on their own journeys.

May all find their truth!

GROWING UP

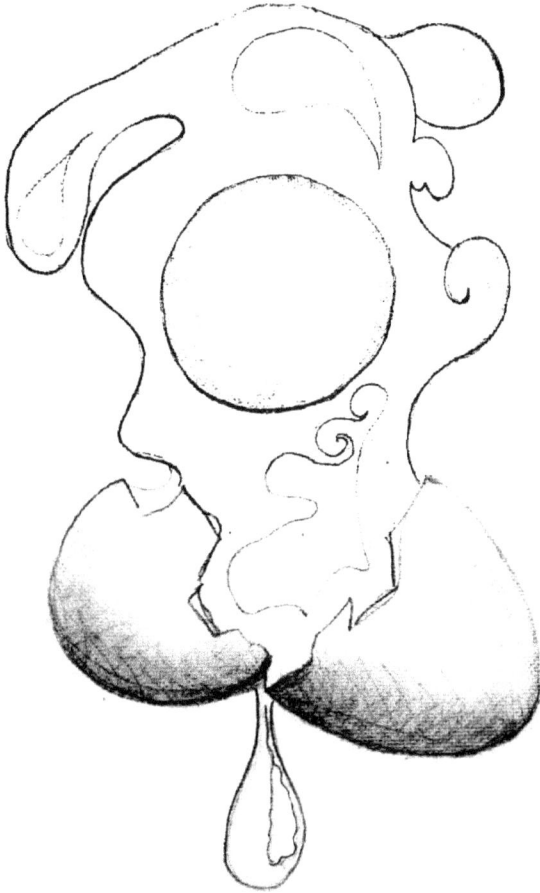

Let me start by saying that I failed my first year of school because my only interest was swinging as high as I could in the playground. I remember the teacher bringing me back to the classroom, and me running back to the swing the moment she turned around. My parents had to transfer me to a different school for the following year and make sure the new school didn't have swings I could reach so easily.

Around age five, I had a dream in which I showed my mother, from above my grave, how I had died from an arrow piercing my heart—a sudden death. This memory remains vivid in my life, as I have been exploring other aspects of my story across different timelines where it might fit, which I will share at a later time.

Throughout the years, I remember having various out-of-body and other such experiences: leaving my physical body while sleeping (flying away or simply floating), and being able to focus single-pointedly on a page I was reading in the middle of a noisy cafeteria, to name a few. I had no friends, as I never felt I belonged anywhere. I preferred talking with people much older than me—especially mature, genuine individuals—and I loved being with animals. I deeply admired and respected nature.

When I was around eight years old, my mother was a member of a yoga group, and she lent me a book about a Tibetan lama written by an English author. As I read it, I had a dream about a group of Tibetan lamas who were in a huge cave performing a ceremony in which I participated. There were several rows of monks chanting. I woke up with an intense wish to meet those lamas. After that, I would sit or lie down in my room, close my eyes, bring my gaze upward, and enter meditation for long periods of time without understanding what I was doing— simply trusting the experience, hoping it would develop into something related with the lamas.

As I entered my teens, my family came to realize we had been victims of witchcraft or some form of black magic. Each of us had struggled with intense challenges that manifested physically—as illness, birth complications, and mental health issues—or simply as an inability to accomplish our goals. My oldest brother lacked the protection of benevolent forces that shielded the rest of us, and his karma seemed marked by hardship. He struggled profoundly with alcohol and drugs throughout his teenage years and young adulthood, which ultimately brought his life to an early end by his own choice.

By then, I had married my first husband. Despite everything, my brother and I always shared a bond of pure love.

Watching my brother struggle the most touched our family to the core. My role shifted from a very early age—I became a source of support for my parents and, to some degree, for my younger brother, especially throughout our childhood and later as adults. I provided different perspectives on situations, helping them heal and move forward. When I connected with Buddhism later in life, I continued to request special prayers and ceremonies to dispel obstructing forces for myself and my family.

The night before he took his life, I had a vivid dream in which he was being chased and cornered by pirates while I tried to help him escape. In an instant, he jumped into a helicopter, and my dream ended. The following morning, I woke up to find that the water tank in the house I shared with my first husband had broken, flooding my garage with clear water. I could feel his energy, his presence. By this time, I had already started to practice Buddhism and was able to request that Phowa practice (transference of consciousness) be performed for him. My mother later had a dream in which he showed her he was living in a beautiful palace, which helped her begin closing a wound that would take years to fully heal.

Returning to my teen years, I became very ill when I was around sixteen. It was a major setback that drained my energy and took several years to overcome. During this dark period, as my parents struggled to help me, protection manifested in the form of a retired doctor who was a friend of one of my father's cousins. He was no ordinary doctor—he was profoundly attuned to the spiritual realm. Since I had been seeking a spiritual path for so long—one my parents had always forbidden—this seemed like a chance to learn something about that dimension of life. It gave me a reason to fight and hold onto a part of myself that had been missing.

At our first meeting, he performed numerology based on my birth date and told me I was special, that he would dedicate all his effort to helping me. I didn't understand what he meant until much later in life, after I contacted a Gypsy friend who helped me confirm and better understand—but that is a story for later on.

After several visits to our house and learning about our family's challenges, he referred us to a woman who practiced white magic, a so-called "white witch". She only agreed to see us given his recommendation, as she lived in hiding, fleeing from black witches who sought revenge for freeing people like us from their dark work.

We were instructed to bring a white egg to the session, purchased from a store, and keep it with us until the appointment. She appeared completely ordinary—a woman in a simple sleeveless dress, light-colored, with no pockets or bags. When my turn came, she guided me to the center of the room. I remember feeling confident in her ability to help us.

I handed her the egg, and she began the session. I recall it being very powerful—I could feel energy surrounding me and something leaving my body. At the end, she cracked the egg before my father and me, and as with the rest of my family, something had materialized inside it.

There was no yolk. Instead, there was evidence of a black witch's work, which corresponded precisely with the type of struggle I had been experiencing; the same was true for each family member. My father tried to find a logical explanation, but none existed. This was something beyond the rational mind—it was meant to be experienced, accepted, and understood through intuition alone.

After that, I began recovering from my illness. As I approached my eighteenth birthday, I was finally allowed to pursue my spiritual search while also choosing a career path and university. I learned some Kabbalah principles from my father—it was a good beginning, but it was not my path. I read many of his books on spirituality, including authors like Madame Blavatsky and others, devouring anything I could find. Still, there was no Buddhism, no sign of Tibetan lamas.

Needless to say, I wasn't popular with other students when I started college, as I was really only interested in meaningful conversations about philosophy or spirituality.

HOW I MET THE TIBETAN LAMAS

While in college, I met my first husband and married shortly before my twenty-first birthday. I followed my intuition—I needed to leave my parents' house to find my spiritual path. Simultaneously, I began working as an intern. Daily life became intense! When my husband accepted a position in Europe, I had the opportunity to visit another continent for the first time—one steeped in history and alive with new adventures.

We stayed about four months working on this project. At that time, I was also hired as an intern. We traveled all over Europe, then returned to Mexico to resume our lives.

I had told my husband about my desire to meet some Tibetan lamas, and to my astonishment, one day, my wish came true. I was working late in an office on the twentieth floor of a building. He came to pick me up, so I asked him to wait in a nearby restaurant. As soon as he arrived at the restaurant, he called to tell me that there were a few Tibetan lamas there.

I abandoned everything and rushed to the restaurant as quickly as possible. He was waiting outside, but when we went inside, there were no lamas. We noticed a long queue at a small theater next door to my office building. When we inquired, we found out that the lamas were inside preparing a ceremony dedicated to the Medicine Buddha.

By the time the program was about to start, no seats remained, so we were invited to sit on the stage behind the row of monks. As the ceremony unfolded, I sat completely still, deeply focused, following the chants in an unfamiliar language and visualizing blue light above my head—the best I could manage, given I had no knowledge of the Medicine Buddha or Tibetan Buddhism.

I remember my entire body began to radiate, as if I had been activated. I felt profoundly joyful, light, alive, filled with a sense of belonging and purpose. It was as though I had finally found what I had been seeking for so long.

I shared this experience with my parents, but my father remained protective. He didn't want to lose his only daughter to a cult, so he asked me to wait and not rush into anything. It took me some time to gather the courage to call Tibet House to inquire about classes. That's when my Buddhist journey truly began.

I managed to attend an introductory course, escorted by my mother. After she confirmed it wasn't a cult, my parents gave me their blessing to carry on. I was eager to study and learn more, but still didn't feel I fully belonged there—my connection was to the teachings themselves. I continued for several years, learning the fundamentals, until I met my first teacher and a Western lama who taught the aforementioned Phowa practice and Mahamudra, or teachings on the nature of mind.

MEETING MY FIRST ROOT TEACHER, THE WESTERN LAMA, AND COMPLETING MY PRELIMINARY PRACTICES

I remember meeting my teacher for the first time in Mexico. He had been invited by the Tibet House. He was deeply compassionate and kind; you could feel his peaceful yet powerful energy field even when he was simply being present. The only challenge was that he lived in Nepal and spoke no English, so I depended on a translator whenever I had the chance to speak with him. I never felt this was an obstacle, which was proven over the years—he would give me brief, pointing out instructions, and I would understand perfectly what he meant.

He visited several times over the years, bestowing empowerments. He had a strong connection with Latin America. He would visit Colombia,

Peru, and Mexico. Students from Guatemala would travel to Mexico when he and another Western lama were teaching.

As for that Western lama, the first time we met, I couldn't stop staring at him, even though I was supposedly conversing with the president and main teacher of Tibet House. I wasn't really paying attention to or even looking at him. The Western lama noticed me from across the room, ran down the stairs, and hugged and kissed me on the cheek. Then we were formally introduced. My first Phowa retreat proved deeply significant— my connection with this practice and any teaching concerning the nature of mind was unmistakable, even though I had minimal understanding of Buddhism, no knowledge of Buddhist rituals or Tantras. I simply practiced Phowa.

A few years passed. At the Tibet House, I received the so-called "Diamond Mind" initiation ritual from a visiting lama, followed by a brief introduction to the practice. When the Western lama visited, I obtained the practice manual and found out that it was a part of the preliminary practices, requiring 100,000 repetitions of each one of the four practices. Without fully comprehending what I was undertaking or whether I could complete so many repetitions, I simply began, applying myself with my limited knowledge.

Later, having acquired more experience and study, I realized that I had completed those preliminary practices out of order—the practice I had started was actually the second of the preliminaries. With this understanding, I repeated the preliminaries in the correct sequence.

With considerable effort, my husband and I traveled to India, Nepal, Thailand, and Hong Kong. It was a magical, liberating experience. I felt at home when visiting sacred Buddhist sites like Lumbini, Bodhgaya, Sarnath, and Tso Pema. In Nepal, we visited my teacher as well as the Swayambhunath and Boudhanath stupas, among other holy places. I remember weeping when I had to leave. The same thing happened on future trips.

Not long after we returned home, a path opened before me: a

semester of study at a Buddhist institute in India. The opportunity came through someone we'd met in Nepal, a translator who had facilitated my conversations with my teacher. I felt the pull unmistakably—I had to return. I was only at the threshold of my journey, with so much yet to discover, especially the practices and teachings that resonated most deeply with me, but couldn't be found in Mexico then.

It was nearly miraculous that I managed to return to India alone. I had to fight to convince my husband, my parents, his parents, and the extended family of aunts, uncles, and others who couldn't understand why I wanted to go to India by myself to study at an institute I had never seen. I was so determined that my husband and parents finally supported me, though they feared losing me forever. We agreed that one semester would give me the experience and knowledge I craved.

Remember those repetitions of the practice I was telling you about? Well, I completed my 100,000 repetitions shortly after arriving in India. I turned thirty at the Buddhist institute, far from my family, which provided me with the space to begin healing from my older brother's recent death. My time there was magical. I felt more at home doing what I truly wanted to do, even though it was only for one semester. It was my first experience of what it meant to be young, to have a group of people who wanted to spend time with me, to be part of a multicultural environment with students from around the world and diverse backgrounds.

The translator who had facilitated my encounters with my teacher, and was now translating classes led by the Tibetan Khenpos (scholars of Buddhist philosophy), introduced me to an extraordinary twelve-year-old girl. She lived in India with her two sisters and parents. We became close friends, and once the school year ended, the girls started spending their days with us at the Buddhist Institute.

They soon became students of my teacher from Nepal as well. Through his blessing, our friendship has endured to this day. She has blossomed into a remarkable young woman—a Buddhist scholar and Tibetan translator for highly respected lamas, among many other accomplishments. More importantly, she would play a profound role in my life years later, when I met my current teacher.

Time passed, and I began working on the first preliminary practice—Refuge with prostrations. I attended the inauguration of my teacher's monastery in Nepal, returned to Tso Pema, inspired by my devotion to Guru Rinpoche, and spent time with other students while attending classes.

When the semester ended, I returned to Mexico to a life that no longer felt like mine. With every penny I saved, I kept returning to the Dharma centers in Europe—primarily Spain and Germany—where I could at least apply myself to the Phowa practices and deepen my understanding of the nature of mind. I obtained the manual for the Refuge preliminary practice, and with that and additional reading, I continued working slowly but steadily.

In Spain, someone gave me her practice text that encompassed all the preliminary practices. I never learned its origin, but it was invaluable. Another person showed me how to perform the mandala offering, and I received the oral transmission (called *lung* in Tibetan) from a lama who traveled with my teacher, allowing me to begin the Guru Yoga practice afterward—the final preliminary practice. I had to absorb as much as possible before returning to Mexico.

During my time in Spain, my husband divorced me. My teacher, with a compassionate yet firm tone, instructed me to return to Mexico for closure. He knew that otherwise I would flee back to India or Nepal and never return!

Following my teacher's instructions, I went back to Mexico to finalize my divorce, starting completely over with no money, no job, and living in my parents' home. I managed to complete my preliminary practices (known as *ngöndro* in the Tibetan language) while simultaneously overcoming numerous obstacles manifesting in various aspects of my life. It was a difficult period, but the blessings of my teacher, the Dharma, and my practice sustained me and kept me company.

Upon completing the preliminaries, I heard of one other person in our small community who had also done the *ngöndro* practices. I was the second person I knew to have completed the preliminary practices in Mexico. I waited, ready for the opportunity to receive the next practice when I could meet again with the Western lama, who was supporting my teacher as he grew increasingly ill.

STARTING MY NEW PRACTICE AND A NEW LIFE

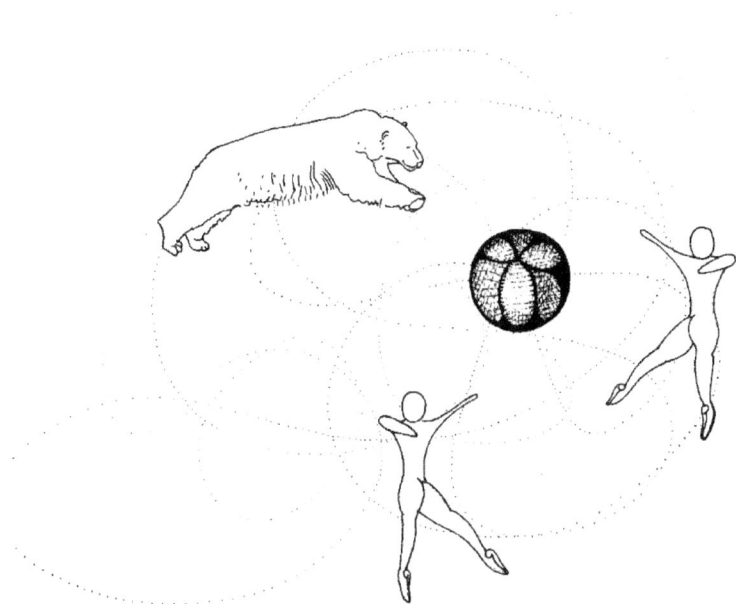

The next Phowa retreat in Mexico arrived, and with it I received my new practice text in the form of photocopies, in English—the proper booklet would only be finalized a few years later. It was precious to me, and with minimal explanation, I eagerly embraced the opportunity to deepen my practice.

By wonderful coincidence, I regained my old position at the building where everything had begun—where I had first met the lamas—and now I was meeting my future husband. We have been together for more than twenty years.

With support from my parents, I slowly rebuilt my life from the ground up. I moved into my 45-square-meter apartment. My boyfriend joined me, and a few months later, with my teacher's blessing, we both applied for positions at our company's U.S. headquarters. We sold everything and embarked on a new life with new jobs in a new country.

Soon after settling in, we married and began the green card application process. We bought our first home. Life accelerated dramatically. Despite everything, I maintained my practice as consistently as possible and continued attending teachings and Phowa or Mahamudra retreats for several years.

I felt stuck in my practice, unable to find the next step. My focus shifted to establishing roots and finding stability so I could heal myself and apply what I had learned from my first marriage. Not long after we bought our house, my husband had to relocate to another state for a new position. Because of the green card process, we decided to maintain our current address. He visited monthly for over a year. Once we received our green cards, we sold the house and moved to his state so we could be together again. My teacher had already passed away, leaving a profound wound in my heart. I was alone again, but as he once told me, always connected, always together. I believe he would have been pleased to know about my new life, my new family.

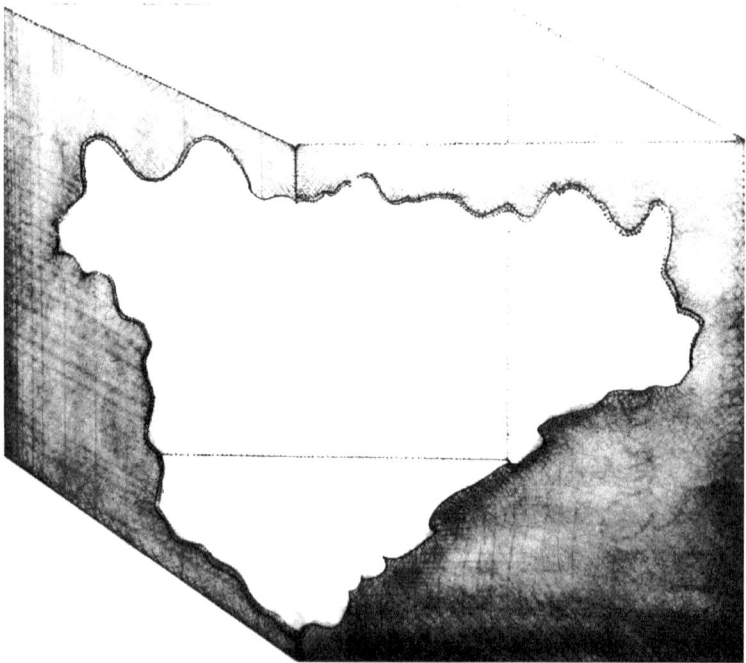

HOW I LEARNED WHAT BEING SPECIAL REALLY MEANT

As a child, I was told several times that I was "special." My father retired while we were young and began studying philosophy, Kabbalah, and other subjects. He asked one of his teachers to create an astrological chart for each of us. I never saw mine, but my parents told me the stars were in my favor.

The yoga group where my mother was now an instructor invited a master who showed great interest in me, though he could sense my connection lay elsewhere.

When I first met my teacher, in one of our initial conversations, I told him about the dream I'd had at age five—how I had died. Years later, through a translator friend, I learned that most of the teachers I had been studying with knew I had a strong connection with Buddhism in past lives, but didn't remember, so they simply let me find my own way.

It felt as though I was never given the chance to choose the life I wanted. I could never claim to know I was special—as a Westerner and a Latin woman, such things are unthinkable; it's not part of our culture. Moreover, how could a Mexican woman born to a non-Buddhist family in a non-Buddhist country be particularly special? And why was I born so far from Buddhism?

Reflecting on this over time, perhaps I didn't want to be easily found, wanting instead to focus on my practice. As far back as I can remember, I have always wanted one thing: to achieve liberation and help others. That has been my birthday wish since I was very young.

Perhaps the conditions to be born near the teachings I most connected with simply didn't arise. Perhaps karmic debts needed to be paid. Perhaps I had not yet found the lineage I was meant to relate to in this current life?

Perhaps I wanted to reach the highest level of realization possible in this life as a Western, Latin woman to inspire other Westerners and give them confidence that it is possible—to trust their own potential.

Or perhaps I simply needed to live the life of a 21st-century Western lay woman practitioner and learn from this experience...

Many years later, I met an extraordinary Gypsy woman—beautiful in every sense—who used my astrological chart and her own divination practices to confirm and expand what I had begun to understand about my past lives. Contemplating why this lifetime had been so unremarkable, I saw connections to a previous existence marked by prolonged rejection and invisibility within a lineage, until finally a Rime master recognized me. Other parallels emerged: stubbornness, confidence, openness, and fearlessness rooted in complete devotion to Guru Rinpoche and, above all, trust in who we truly are. I discovered other connections as well—outer, inner, and secret—which I choose to keep to myself.

HOW I MET MY PRESENT TEACHERS

Years passed, and the feeling of being stuck remained persistent. I was practicing and receiving teachings, yet something was still missing, and I couldn't identify what. I reconnected with my dear friend from India to work on my very basic Tibetan. By wonderful coincidence, she had relocated to the United States.

During our time together, I explained my need to grow in my practice and understanding of Dharma. She suggested I attend teachings from her teachers. That's how I had the privilege of meeting my current teachers—highly accomplished, powerful spiritual leaders under whose guidance I now study and practice.

I began attending yearly retreats and online teachings, and that feeling of being stuck dissolved. I was once again joyful and grateful for the depth of the teachings and practices I was learning. Spending time with my teachers was invaluable and gave me the courage over the years to share my story. As I was listening to my teachers' stories, memories from the time I had traveled to Europe to receive teachings started to awaken in me. I remember attending a four-day retreat in Germany where, on an external level, I faced several difficulties. My tent arrived without poles, leaving me without shelter. Every night, I had to sleep in a different place, carrying my backpack with all my belongings everywhere I went.

However, that brief four-day retreat overflowed with blessings and teachings from a very special Rinpoche from Nepal, with whom we had held other retreats to accumulate mantras. During the empowerment, seeds were planted that would later flourish with my new teacher. On the final day of the retreat, the head of the lineage came and gave us the oral transmission of the practice.

On the last night of the retreat, I decided to sleep on the floor with my head pointing toward the chair where the lineage holder had sat. I dreamed of a pair of black crows standing at the doors of the residence where he was sleeping. Unbeknownst to me, profound blessings were already weaving the path that would lead me to my present teachers. A year later, during my final visit while circumambulating the new temple, a pair of black crows appeared day after day, then disappeared as if they had never been. This sacred omen confirmed the path had guided me to where the next chapter must unfold

WHAT'S NEXT...

After this long journey, looking back at all the hardships and struggles, there have been countless blessings and protection through my profound devotion and connection with Guru Rinpoche and the Buddha—trusting my path, guided by them through my intuition and the power of never giving up.

There have been moments when I doubted myself, and during those times, they manifested very vividly—present as an energy field surrounding me, clear images confirming this is my truth, not my imagination. Their protection and care have manifested in various ways, such as through a vajra brother who, through his strong empathic intuition, told me exactly what I needed to hear in that moment: "You are not crazy."

As for what comes next, the need to communicate my experiences and the lessons learned along the way has manifested through several messages arriving at different times. I felt compelled to tell my story. I see this brief narrative as the completion of one cycle—by understanding my past, I can release what no longer serves any purpose and focus all my energy on the present to fulfill my promises and wishes with complete confidence. There is still so much to accomplish.

I chose to share these aspects of my story as a form of healing and closure, creating space for a new cycle where I am more at peace, where I feel more integrated with myself and the world, despite the dark times we are living in. I also know there is a gift to the world hidden in my heart, to be released when the time is right—most likely in a future life. My Guru pointed this out several times. My only wish is that I am ready and that it brings benefit on all levels to all beings.

I close by stating that I am happily married to a husband who supports my pursuit of the Dharma. I have found a wealth of Dharma teachings that have opened new dimensions and understanding in my journey. I am ready to face what comes next with an open heart full of devotion, confidence, and gratitude.

I supplicate my Guru, the Buddha, and my teachers: through their kindness and wisdom, may the wishes of all who encounter this sincere story come true. May they find their path, and may it be full of blessings, protection, and accomplishments.

I completed this text without prior planning, on the second of October of 2025, which coincides with the anniversary of Guru Nyima Ozer, one of Guru Rinpoche's manifestations, on the tenth day of the month of the Pig, in the year of the Wood Snake.

THREE PRAYERS FROM MY HEART

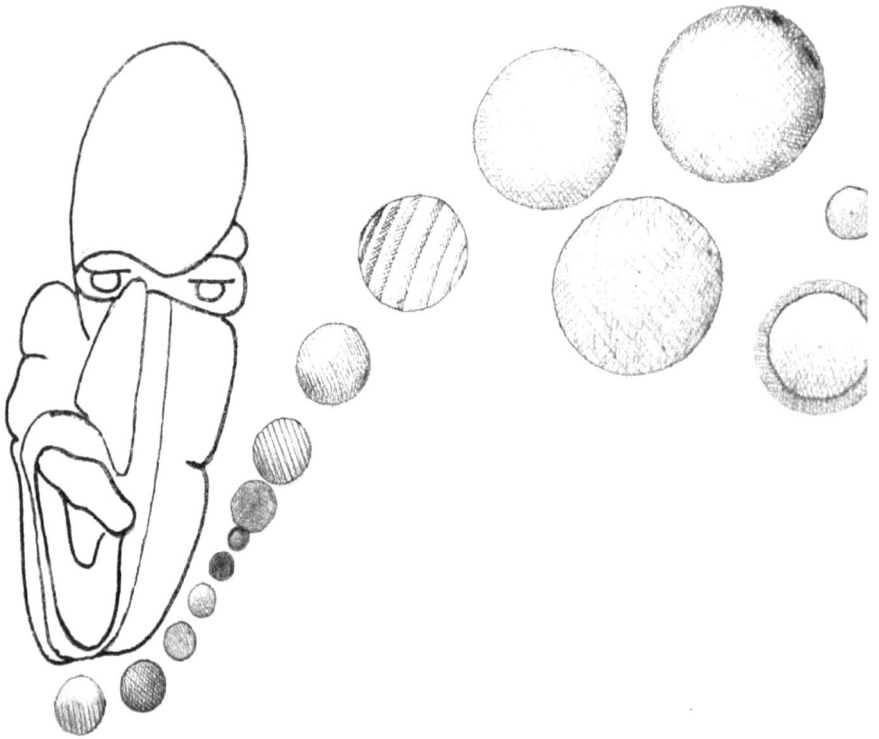

A SINCERE PRAYER THAT COMES FROM THE HEART

May the ocean of existence and the essence of beings
Be touched by a downpour of blessings
And the thunder of luminosity
Dispel the darkness and bring all beings to their natural state

By the power of the awakened mind
May those dwelling in the three bardos
Find refuge in the pure realm of Sukhavati or
Be born with the conditions to benefit and
Protect this world and its inhabitants

By the power of this aspiration
May they [the beings and the environment] be healed?
From any disease of the three doors, pollution, poisons, and the like,
And may the conditions for peace, stability, well-being, and a conducive
environment arise effortlessly.

May all be auspicious!

I, Tashi Paldron, composed this aspiration prayer on the 24th of March 2024, out of deep devotion to my all-pervading Guru and with profound gratitude, as an offering to the precious Buddha of this time, my nirmanakaya Gurus, my mothers, and my sisters, in hopes that it inspires and benefits others.

February 3, 2025

Emaho!
How fortunate you are, child of the Noble Family,
Abiding single-pointedly and without distraction
In the Dhatu

Taking refuge in the three jewels, the three roots,
With bodhicitta and dedicating merit, all within
A single instant, inseparable from the Guru

Enjoying the one taste of all appearances,
This yogini abides unmoved, confident, and Fearless

May all beings become liberated at once!

I, Tashi Paldron, composed this short prayer while in retreat, with gratitude to my ever-present Guru, the source of all refuges. May it bring benefit to all.

THE YEAR 2025, DAYS BEFORE THE
NO KING'S PROTESTS

Precious Guru Rinpoche

Protect all beings from the powers

That destroy the world and the environment

Destroy themselves and destroy each other

I, Tashi Paldron, composed this supplication in light of the events happening in these times (year of 2025).

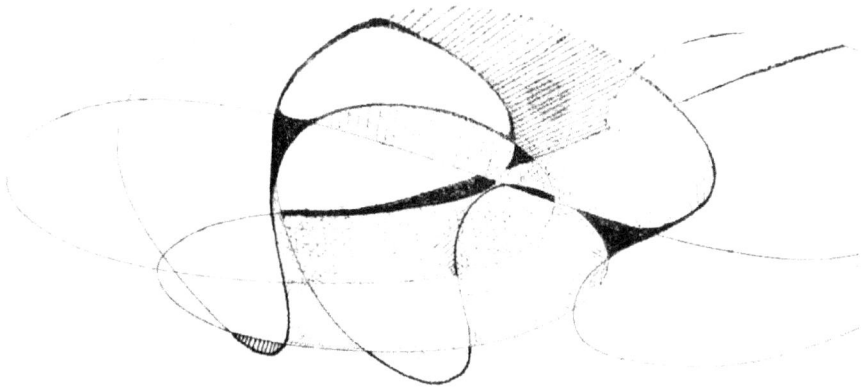

.

www.ingramcontent.com/pod-product-compliance
Lightning Source LLC
LaVergne TN
LVHW051807080426
835511LV00019B/3436